FORD
ABOMI-
NATION

FORD ABOMI-NATION

LINWOOD BARCLAY

DOUG FORD STEERS ONTARIO RIGHT — **INTO THE DITCH**

ECW

Published by ECW Press
665 Gerrard Street East
Toronto, Ontario, Canada M4M 1Y2
416-694-3348 / info@ecwpress.com

Cover design: David A. Gee
Cartoons: Brian Gable/The Globe and Mail

LIBRARY AND ARCHIVES CANADA CATALOGUING IN PUBLICATION

Title: Ford abomination / Linwood Barclay.

Names: Barclay, Linwood, author.

Identifiers: Canadiana (print) 20190166495
Canadiana (ebook) 20190166525

ISBN 9781770415508 (softcover)
ISBN 9781773054575 (PDF)
ISBN 9781773054568 (ePUB)

Subjects: LCSH: Ford, Doug, 1964—Humor. | LCSH: Politicians—Ontario—Humor. | LCSH: Premiers (Canada)—Ontario—Humor. | CSH: Ontario—Politics and government—2003—Humor.

Classification: LCC FC3061.3 .B37 2019
DDC 971.3/0500207—dc23

The publication of *Ford AbomiNation* has been generously supported by the Government of Canada. *Ce livre est financé en partie par le gouvernement du Canada.* We acknowledge the support of the Government of Ontario through Ontario Creates for the marketing of this book.

PRINTED AND BOUND IN CANADA

PRINTING: COPYWELL 5 4 3 2 1

"I give you my word: Not one single person will be laid off when I become premier."

— DOUG FORD

Bland works!
PREMIER BILL DAVIS 1971-85
HELLO
PROGRESSIVE CONSERVATIVE
PARTY OF ONTARIO!!!
DOUG
FORD
GABLE

INTRODUCTION

Just slightly more than twenty years ago, I wrote a book called *Mike Harris Made Me Eat My Dog*. This tome — it was also more than a hundred pages! — was a serious political examination of that Ontario premier's Progressive Conservative administration and its policies. One might go so far as to call it scholarly.

You could tell it was a serious book because it had footnotes.[1]

Mike Harris, a one-time teacher from North Bay who

1 Here's one now! But the book did not, I must confess, have a bibliography. Not just because I didn't know where to put all the periods and semicolons, but because I never expected anyone to get to the end and notice. Also, no index. Too much work.

went on to become a member of the Ontario provincial legislature and then the leader of his party, campaigned on something called the Common Sense Revolution, where "common sense" was defined as driving around the city of Toronto all night trying to find an emergency ward that could treat you.

During the Harris years, the people of Ontario went through massive cutbacks to education, which precipitated a massive, province-wide teacher strike. Several hospitals were closed, but that was okay, because hundreds of nurses had been laid off.[2] Cuts to welfare increased homelessness and poverty levels. Projects to repair crumbling infrastructure were scrapped. The various municipalities that made up Metro Toronto were forced to merge, bringing about mass confusion and less local accountability. Boot camps were set up to deal with youthful offenders.

Oh yeah, and deregulation of water testing and cuts to the Ministry of Environment were found to be partly responsible for an entire town's water supply getting poisoned.

People died.

Is it any wonder that, twenty years later, the good people of Ontario were getting somewhat wistful? Were

---

2 He likened nurses to makers of hula hoops: they were obsolete. True story. I shit you not.

those great times, or what? Was there any way we could get to relive that magnificent period?

So in 2018, Ontarians elected another Progressive Conservative, Doug Ford, a politician whose resumé included a degree from Trump University, as their premier.

Now, to help explain how Ontario got to this point, it's worth looking at what happened in the intervening years. Mike Harris decided to call it quits and handed things over to a guy named Ernie Eves, who, with his slicked-back hair and pinstriped suits, looked like a 1920s Chicago gangster. But despite his tough appearance, he was a bit of a softy, at least compared to Mike, so the cons didn't like him as much. A less abrasive style might have been designed to win back those who'd been affected adversely by Mike's take-no-prisoners approach,[3] but it didn't work.

Teachers and principals and nurses and doctors and labour leaders and every single person who either worked for the province or had to deal with any staff-slashed provincial agency was not in a mood to forgive the party for what it had done.

When the next election came around, Ernie was toast.

The Liberals got in, led by Dalton McGuinty, who looked exactly like Anthony Perkins from *Psycho* but

3 Like, everyone.

had less personality. McGuinty was, in a word, *nice*, and for several years, there was relative peace across the land. He was "Ontario's Dad," an image his opponents, curiously, tried to use to smear him. It was like trying to drum up a mob, armed with pitchforks and torches, to run Ward Cleaver out of town because he didn't send Beaver to one of those boot camps.

But behind the scenes, Dalton[4] was making all sorts of mistakes. One of his biggest was moving a proposed gas plant out of Oakville at a cost of hundreds of millions of dollars, all to win a local seat. There were other gaffes. Hydro costs were out of control. Aides destroyed emails to cover up political shenanigans. And, generally, people were just getting tired of him.

So, Dalton decided to pack it in and go into the witness protection program. There was one reported sighting of him in a Wendy's in Duluth, Minnesota, in April 2017, but it's now believed that may have actually been Elvis.

Dalton turned over his mess to Kathleen Wynne, a former education minister, and she managed to keep the Liberal boat afloat for a few more years until it took on

---

4 The word "dalton" was adopted as a unit of measurement for disappointment. For example, not getting your newspaper in the morning would be two daltons, while having your dog run over by a FedEx truck would be eight.

so much water that the Ontario electorate, desperate to get rid of her, would have voted for someone with the IQ of a Canadian Shield rock sample.

Which some would argue is what happened.

Before he expressed an interest in running the province, Doug Ford's greatest claim to fame was as the brother of Rob Ford, who was, for a period of time, an internationally famous mayor of Toronto.[5] Doug was a city councillor, handing out twenties to constituents in Etobicoke, and while he lived very much in his brother's shadow during that time, he clearly harboured much greater ambitions.

But there wasn't much he could do about it. The Progressive Conservatives had a leader, Patrick Brown, to take them into the next election, which was only a few months away. But then Brown was accused of extreme creepiness and forced out of the job. (The scandal faded away, and Brown became mayor of Brampton, which is somewhere outside of Toronto, although no one knows exactly where.)

When he first started making noise about seeking the leadership of the Ontario Progressive Conservative party, many were skeptical. Yeah, right, like Doug's going to get

5 So far as we know, the only Toronto mayor to do Jimmy Kimmel's show.

that job, when there are some other very talented, high-profile contenders, like Christine Elliott, the Whitby-Oshawa MPP for nine years, and Caroline Mulroney, the daughter of former prime minister Brian Mulroney, whose vast political experience consisted of being the daughter of former prime minister Brian Mulroney.

But the last few years have taught us that presenting yourself as someone knowledgeable and intelligent is a much overrated strategy. You say you went to Harvard? You've done a TED Talk? You speak ten languages? So what? The other guy's promising beer for a buck!

How do you beat that?[6]

So, Doug Ford is now the premier of Ontario, the second largest province in the country and the most heavily populated, unless you count trees, which are on his hit list. His decisions directly impact the lives of nearly 13.5 million people, or nearly 40 percent of the country. And he is going to be in this job for at least the next two or three years.

Maybe even more after that.

Those who support his agenda could not be happier. If you've been wondering whether you're one of those people, a member of the so-called Ford Nation — those regular, down-to-earth Ontarians who think Doug is

---

6 Pot for a penny?

the best thing since a party pack of Timbits — you might find the following list helpful.

IF YOU'RE ON THIS LIST, YOU ARE NOT FORD NATION MATERIAL

High school student, high school teacher, elementary school student, elementary school teacher, a parent of a student in any Ontario public school, a librarian, someone who uses libraries, someone who understands how to operate a book, a kid who comes to school hungry and is hoping someone will give him something to eat so he can stay awake until 11 a.m., an autistic child, a parent of an autistic child, a resident of Toronto, a Northern Ontario firefighter, a tree, a species on any endangered list (e.g., a Conservative MPP with an ounce of self-respect), a colonoscopy patient who would prefer not to be awake when someone shoves a camera up their ass, a nurse or any other provincial health care worker, a person who needs the help of a nurse or any other provincial health care worker, a low-income person facing charges who desperately needs legal aid, someone who thinks appointees to top provincial jobs should be qualified, a person who likes to breathe air that does not smell like it just came out of the back end of a Greyhound bus, an Ontarian whose first language is French and does not have a seizure upon seeing a sign that says ARRÊT, an advocate for sex education that goes beyond telling a child that dancing leads to eternal damnation.

In the chapters that follow, you'll find a thoughtful, reasoned examination of the various policy initiatives that the Ford administration has been working on since taking over at Queen's Park.

Also, cartoons.

Think of this book as *Mike Harris Made Me Eat My Dog: The Sequel, Part Deux*.

That's pretty much what the citizens of Ontario feel they're going through.

CAMPAIGN ADS
I LOVE ELECTION YEARS!

CHAPTER ONE

IN A SECRET THINK TANK, THE SCIENTISTS GOT TO WORK . . .

Every great superhero has an origin story. Peter Parker is bitten by a radioactive spider and becomes Spider-Man. Bruce Banner is exposed to massive amounts of gamma radiation and turns into the Hulk. Reed Richards and his friends became the Fantastic Four after their rocket is bombarded by cosmic rays.

And then there is Doug Ford.

It's not a stretch to say that Doug Ford, at least to those on the right who support him and his policies, is seen that way, minus the cape and the tights.[7]

7 For the image I have just planted in your head, you're welcome.

There's much we know about Doug Ford's background, and a bit that we don't.

What we do know is Doug grew up in the Etobicoke part of Toronto and that as a young man he went to work for Deco Labels and Tags, the company his father co-founded. We know he eventually succeeded his father as president of the business.

Doug got a seat on Toronto City Council in 2010 and championed cost-cutting moves, including slashing budgets for city libraries. It became clear that, throughout his life, most of Doug Ford's reading has consisted of labels and tags and little else. He bragged that if author Margaret Atwood were to walk right past him, he wouldn't know who she was, and this was no doubt a relief for Atwood, who might have felt obliged to talk to him had he said hello.

Ford ran for mayor in 2014, and while he lost to John Tory, he got a huge whack of the vote. Supposedly, he went back to running Deco Labels. In September 2017, he announced that he would try once again to become mayor of Toronto, but these plans changed when Patrick Brown was ousted as the provincial Conservative leader.

But what happened between November 2014 and September 2017? Was Doug just running the label company, printing thousands of little sticky notes that read "Toronto Sucks"? Or was something else going on?

It was around this time that a top-secret research project was underway in a right-wing, western Canadian think tank.[8] Delegates from across the country had gathered to find the perfect candidate to lead the conservative cause in Ontario.

But what if the perfect candidate could not be found? What if the perfect candidate did not exist?

Well, said one of the people in the tank, then maybe we'll just have to build one.

While politicians on the right are often skeptical of science,[9] they were willing to make an exception in this case. A team of scientists was brought in. A laboratory was set up in one end of the think tank.

The plan?

Collect DNA samples from the leaders they most admired. One from Mike Harris. Samples from everyone who worked at The Rebel Media. If he would agree to provide one, a sample from Donald Trump himself. (He

---

8 A little background on right-wing think tanks: They are shaped roughly like railway tanker cars, but without wheels, and have walls that are constructed of six-inch steel. There are no windows. This way, no light from the outside world gets in, and it is impossible, once you're inside, to hear any points of view that might conflict, in any way, with the statistics that you're making up.

9 "Global warming, seriously? I just had to get a new plug-in block heater for my F-150."

went along with the idea.[10]) They even got someone in England to find one of Margaret Thatcher's old hairbrushes.

As the scientists were working to combine these various strands of DNA,[11] they realized that all their beakers and microscopes and everything else in the lab were not adequately labelled. The last thing anyone wanted was a mix-up.

"Can anyone recommend," one scientist asked, "a really good label maker?"

The call went out to Deco. Realizing instantly that this think tank was a valuable new client with the potential for lots of future business, Doug Ford himself flew out, taking all his labelling equipment with him.

"I understand your needs," he told the scientists. "You're in good hands."

Things went well, at first.

Doug printed out a whack of labels, including:

HARRIS DNA
TRUMP DNA

---

10 However, a second sample — a drop of blood — became necessary. The first sample provided was a lock of hair, but once the researchers began to work on it, they could not determine that it was any substance known to science.

11 Think one of those shaky things at the paint store.

REBEL DNA
DNA COMBO
COFFEE MACHINE
CREAM
SUGAR
BOYS ONLY! GIRLS KEEP OUT!

He made sure they were all stuck on, and that increases in think-tank heat, humidity, and hot air (especially) would not cause them to peel off. He could not wait for the scientists to come back and see what he had done.

As they entered the lab, Ford swung his arms wide and said, "Check it out!"

But his left arm accidentally hit the DNA COMBO beaker, which was full of all those samples combined. It began to wobble off its stand. Ford turned quickly to catch it but tripped on his own feet. He fell to the floor, and the beaker came with him.

Later, the scientists said it was just like in a movie. It all seemed to happen in slow motion.

The beaker tipped, spilling its contents. Ford landed on his back and looked up as the DNA splashed all over his face. Some of it landed in his mouth. Some of it dribbled up into his nostrils.

Doug quickly sat up, wiped his face.

"Yuck," he said.

But everyone else froze. No one dared approach.

They were . . . waiting.

"What's the problem?" Doug asked. "I'm fine. I'm perfectly fi— "

Now it was Doug's turn to freeze. His eyes bugged out. He appeared to have stopped breathing.

"We have to call an ambulance," one scientist said, unable to hide the panic in his voice.

"No, wait," said another, very cautiously. "Let's . . . see what happens."

Slowly, Doug turned to look at them. His eyes were glazed. He appeared to be looking straight through them. But then, slowly, he got to his feet, as if in a trance. Then he just stood there.

"Mr. Ford?" a scientist said.

Doug Ford mumbled something.

"What was that?"

Doug Ford mumbled again.

"Are you saying 'bug a bear'? Why would you want us to bug a bear? That's not a very safe thing to do."

Slowly, Doug shook his head from side to side. "Buck a beer," he said, this time more articulately.

"Buck a beer?"

"Buck a beer! Buck a beer!"

The future premier began to say the phrase faster and faster.

"Buck a beer! Buck a beer! Buck a beer! Buck a beer! Buck a beer! Buck a beer! Buck a beer! Buck a beer! Buck a beer! Buck a beer!"

The scientists ran to find the heads of the think tank. When they got to the lab and saw what had happened, they could not conceal their excitement.

"You've done it!" they cried. "It's ALIVE!"

The rest, as they say, is history.

THE PEOPLE HAVE SPOKEN...
THE PEOPLE
Government of Ontario
Public Policy Du Jour
GABLE GLOBE&MAIL

CHAPTER TWO

PICKING YOUR TEAM, OR GETTING UNEMPLOYED LACROSSE PLAYERS BACK TO WORK

Doug Ford ran into a little trouble when he tried to make his good buddy Ron Taverner the new head of the Ontario Provincial Police.

In his seventies, an age when many have embraced retirement, Taverner was a superintendent with the Toronto police who'd worked the Etobicoke beat for years and years, so he and Doug were pretty tight. The problem with putting him in the top OPP job was that, well, Taverner, on paper, did not exactly meet the qualifications. He had not served at a high-enough level in the police hierarchy to be eligible for the job that Ford wanted to put him in.

Not a problem.

Before the appointment was announced, the job requirements were quietly changed. Relaxed, as it were. This is more or less the reverse of what those Hollywood celebrity types did when they got their kids into Ivy League colleges by getting ringers to write their entrance exams. What Ford did was more akin to those colleges waiving the exams altogether.

Now, in a normal administration, this is the sort of thing that might be frowned upon. Suppose one day there are allegations that the premier has done something illegal. You really think one of his closest friends is going to investigate him?

But wait a minute. Isn't that why the appointment makes perfect sense?

Sadly for Ford, picking Taverner raised quite a ruckus, and the superintendent excused himself from the running. The entire affair raised plenty of questions about how this premier picks people for top-tier jobs.

Eventually, the Taverner affair faded from the headlines. But several months later, there was a sequel.

The premier's chief of staff, a gentleman by the name of Dean French, appointed two people to "agents-general" positions in New York and London, jobs that paid more than $150,000 a year. One was known to French through their mutual participation in lacrosse, and the other was a second cousin to French's wife. Once news broke about these appointments, Ford rescinded them, and French resigned.

Not only was this terribly unfair to those two people who had their new gigs pulled out from under them, it was a huge setback in the government's mandate to find work for members of the lacrosse community. As most people know, it is not easy to find full-time work when most of your experience is wielding a stick with a little net at the end of it.

But you have to ask yourself: What is the point of getting into a position of power if you can't use it to reward those closest to you? Isn't that the reason people seek high office, or work with those who do? To live a life of privilege and to share it with your pals?

This is not to say that the Ford government doesn't consider each and every job applicant, across all its various ministries, with the utmost seriousness. That's why it has drawn up a new employment questionnaire in a bid to find the best possible people.

ONTARIO GOVERNMENT JOB APPLICATION QUESTIONNAIRE

Please fill in the following:

Name: ______________________________

Address: ______________________________

Email address: ______________________________

Phone number: ______________________________

D.O.B.: ______________________________

Favourite barbecue sauce: ______________________________

Favourite beer: ______________________________

Favourite lacrosse player: ______________________________

All-time favourite Toronto mayor: ______________________________

What kind of 4WD vehicle do you own? ______________________________

Multiple-Choice Section

1. The exhaust fumes spewing out the back of a car:

    a) smell like victory
    b) help to remind you, when walking away from the vehicle, whether you left the car running or not
    c) look especially pretty in the winter
    d) all of the above

2. Standing ovations in the legislature are given only when:

    a) the premier says something brilliant
    b) the premier says something moderately brilliant
    c) the premier says something so dumb you want to slap your forehead so hard you go unconscious; in other words, whenever the premier's lips move
    d) all of the above

3. When cornered in a Queen's Park hallway by a reporter asking tough questions:

a) play dead
b) pull closest fire alarm
c) pepper spray
d) all of the above

4. Now that the slogan on provincial licence plates is changing from "Yours to Discover" to "A Place to Grow,"[12] what other traditional symbols of Ontario should be changed?

a) the official flower, the white trillium, should be changed to asphalt because everything looks prettier when it's flat
b) the official tree, the eastern white pine, should be changed to a Home Depot two-by-four-by-eight
c) the official animal, the common loon, should be changed to — wait, that seems more perfect than ever
d) all of the above

We don't want to give away too much here, but if you selected (d) for all four of those questions, you just might be the kind of person we're looking for. But there's more.

---

12 "A Place for Grow-Ops" was a close second, but some feared it was too much of a reminder of the premier's formative years.

Skill-Testing Question

If you would not characterize yourself as a close friend or associate of Doug Ford, the following question, which you must answer within thirty seconds without the aid of a calculator, is for you:

> Determine the square root of the number you get after multiplying 34,986 by 8,976 and dividing that number by .00965.

If you are, in fact, a close friend or associate of Doug Ford, the following question, which you may take home and bring back tomorrow, is for you:

> Spell BEER.

Finally

On a scale of 1 to 10, how would you rate your level of self-respect, with "1" meaning you believe you are pond scum and "10" meaning you have principles, you don't tolerate fools gladly, and you are willing to speak your mind in the face of authority even if the consequences could be serious?

If you said "1," we'll be in touch.

This seems like as good a time as any to set the record straight on a campaign slogan that the Ford team put out during the 2018 election.

You may remember it: "For the People."

It was on signs and buttons and pamphlets and bumper stickers. But there was a mistake at the printers. A minor typo.

Given all the appointments that have been doled out to associates and relatives of the Doug Ford administration, it's now apparent that the slogan was supposed to be slightly different. Word is it will be fixed to the following for the next election, accompanied by photos of Doug and his friends:

"For **THESE** People"

GABLE/GLOBE+MAIL
FORD TOWER
WE LIVE IN INTERESTING TIMES.
THE FORD DOME
LAKE FORD
FORD ISLANDS
THE FORDINER EXPRESSWAY
FORD SHORE BLVD

CHAPTER THREE

HOORAY FOR DOUGIEWOOD!

Who needs a meddlesome CBC? Who needs nosy parkers like Matt Galloway on *Metro Morning* or John Moore on Newstalk 1010 or Susan Delacourt from the *Toronto Star*? Who needs any of those annoying investigative reporters from the *Globe and Mail*?

They can all go piss up a rope.

If you are Doug Ford or one of his minions, you'd have to be out of your mind to agree to an interview with any of these people or anyone else from their news outlets. You don't need them! You can get your message out on your own — unfiltered!

You have countless social media platforms. You've got your Facebook. You've got your Twitter. You've got your own websites where you can get your point across. You can hire your own reporters (sorry, *actors*) to ask you questions! This is how real journalism was always meant to be.

Here's how it used to be done:

PREMIER: I'm here today, standing on this spot, to announce $500 million to build a new hospital!

REPORTER: Mr. Premier, wasn't it the previous government that set aside the $500 million to build this new hospital?

PREMIER: *(befuddled)* Um, uh, okay, *that* $500 million —

At this point, the premier's aide would move him away from the podium and shove him into the back of a waiting limo, which would then zoom off, tires squealing.

Here's how it is done now:

PREMIER: I'm here today, standing on this spot, to announce $500 million to build a new hospital!

PRETEND REPORTER: Would it seem forward to ask if we can kiss your magnificent ass as a show of our gratitude?

Are you an aspiring journalist who'd like to maybe, one day, interview the premier himself? Do you want to get into the real nuts and bolts of how Ontario is run, how decisions are made, how a provincial government that is larger than many nations gets things done on a daily basis, how partisanship is damaging to the electorate, how petty political squabbles do little to forward the public's interests?

If the answers to those questions are a resounding *YES!*, then maybe you should think about becoming a journalist someplace else. But if you want to report for Ford TV and get a sit-down with the top dog, here are some sample questions (if yours are different, you're going to have to submit them in advance) that we just know the premier will be happy to field:

- ☐ "Snowmobiling or jet-skiing? Which have you found to be more delightfully damaging to natural habitats?"
- ☐ "Oh my God, you look great! How much weight have you lost?"
- ☐ "Would you like to see Kathleen Wynne sent to the gulag, or another planet, and if the latter, which one? Is a breathable atmosphere an issue?"
- ☐ "Which three people would you most like to have dinner with and they're all Donald Trump, aren't they?"
- ☐ "Did I mention that you look terrific? Have you been working out?"

The Ford administration not only has its own online news show to hammer home its various messages, it is now a firmly established network in its own right. It has a full slate of programs designed not only to inform Ontarians but to entertain them. Tune in for shows like:

The Walking Dead of QP: What's it like to be a Progressive Conservative backbencher? The premier and the members of his cabinet get all the attention, but what about the lives of his backbench MPPs? Don't they deserve a little attention, too? Each week this gripping reality show follows a day-in-the-life of a different back-bench MPP. We see them tackle the kinds of tasks the premier is willing to trust them with: sharpening pencils, cleaning the whitewalls on the premier's special SUV,[13] picking up his dry cleaning.

Kim's Inconvenience: The owner of a variety store located a block from Queen's Park must endure a constant parade of Liberal and NDP MPPs coming in and clearing him out of antacid tablets.

Schitt Show: This concerns a province that —[14]

And kids aren't being forgotten either. What preschooler won't want to park herself in front of the TV every morning to watch *Mr. Messup*, where the premier will stick his hand up the butts of his MPPs and make them say whatever the hell he wants.

---

13 More about that later!

14 Seriously? You need a joke for this one?

And for out and out laughs, there's a terrific new situation comedy coming called *Those Darn Species!* The show is built around a big-time developer named Frug Dord, who has projects underway throughout the province. Every week, some new, pesky, whacky environmentalist, who says Dord's latest project will wipe out some species that no one really cares about anyway (barn owl, wood turtle, boreal caribou, etc.), tries to step in the way of progress. But each episode ends happily when Dord is given permission by the province to wipe out a species in return for a modest fee.

But one of the most popular shows, right from the beginning, has been the game show *Wheel of Misfortune*, running every night on Ford TV right after the dinner hour. Here's a clip from one of the earlier episodes, back when Victor Fedeli was *still* minister of finance, and Lisa MacLeod was *still* minister of community and social services, and Laurie Scott was *still* minister of labour:[15]

FORD: Good evening and welcome to *Wheel of Misfortune*, where Conservative cabinet members compete to see who can claw back the most money from an Ontario special interest group. Our returning champion is Victor Fedeli. Joining him today are Lisa

---

15 For a complete list of former Ford government cabinet ministers, see *Ford AbomiNation*, Volume 2, coming in 2020.

MacLeod and Laurie Scott, minister of labour. As our returning champ, Victor, you go first and spin the wheel.

FEDELI: Thanks, Premier! Here goes!

(wheel goes tick-tick-tick)

FORD: Oh, you've landed on minus five hundred dollars. Choose a letter.

FEDELI: Is there a U?

FORD: Yes. *(ding!)* There's a U! Christine Elliott, our minister of health,[16] could I get you to turn that letter over for us?

ELLIOTT: *(under her breath)* I've never been so humiliated in my life.

FORD: Victor, you want to solve?

FEDELI: Uh, I think I'll spin.

(wheel goes tick-tick-tick, followed by a sour trumpet sound)

FORD: Oh no! You've landed on "Help the Disadvantaged" and must forfeit your turn! Over to you, Lisa.

MACLEOD: Let's do this!

(wheel goes tick-tick-tick)

FORD: You've landed on minus $1,000! Way to go, Lisa. Pick a letter.

---

16 As I write this, but who knows.

MACLEOD: Is there a K?

FORD: One K! Christine, you want to flip that over?

ELLIOTT: You bet! *(under her breath)* I'll flip you the bird, that's what I'd like to flip. A lifetime of public service and now I have to do the bidding of someone with the IQ of a —

FORD: Did you say something, Christine?

ELLIOTT: I just said, I've cued up the letters. Good to go!

FORD: You want to solve the puzzle, Lisa?

MACLEOD: *(pondering)* I . . . don't think so. I'll spin.

(wheel goes tick-tick-tick, followed by a sour trumpet sound)

FORD: Tough break. You've landed on "Cut Class Sizes." Looks like it's finally your turn, Laurie.

SCOTT: I think I know it.

FORD: You've got to spin the wheel first!

SCOTT: You bet!

(wheel goes tick-tick-tick)

SCOTT: Yes! Yes!

FORD: Yes, that's cause for celebration! You've landed on minus $1 million. Pick a letter.

SCOTT: Is there a C?

FORD: There *is* a C! Christine? Where did Christine go? Oh well, I can tell you it's the last letter in the first word. Do you want to solve the puzzle?

SCOTT: Autistic kids!

FORD: Yes!

(Christine wanders back on stage, reveals all the letters, flipping them so hard some of them hit the floor)

FORD: Congratulations, Laurie. Because you had a million dollars riding on this, that's how much we're cutting from programs to help autistic kids. Okay, let's start with a new phrase.

If ever there was a guaranteed hit, this is it.

Finally, one has to wonder why Doug Ford needs his own news network when the established media have served him so well. He's a master of the bait and switch, of drawing your attention over here while he does something over there. Beer for a buck, tailgate parties, stickers for gas pumps: these are all shiny little objects that dazzle and distract the media and smartass writers, like the one who's written the very book you're reading.

That's why if Doug Ford is going to do something Ontarians will really hate, it's best to announce it on the same day as something quirky. Float some crazy idea you might never even implement so that the press will take their collective eye off the ball.

That's why you see headline juxtapositions like these:

BEER IN SCHOOL CAFETERIAS?

HOSPITALS ELIMINATED

Brilliant, yes?

ON THE BRIGHT SIDE... WE'VE GOT SEX EDUCATION WELL UNDER CONTROL.
Shootings Shootings Shootings
ONTARIO
GLOBE+MAIL-GABLE

CHAPTER FOUR

THE DIRTY STUFF

Back when Doug Ford was growing up, things were simple.

There were boys, and there were girls. And there were some fancy boys who always tried out for the lead in the high school musical, and some girls who showed a strange affinity for auto shop. But on the whole, the boy-girl dynamic was pretty straightforward. She might say no, but you knew, in her heart, she meant yes. It was great if your dad had a station wagon. And if you pulled out in time, she wouldn't get pregnant.

And there was no #MeToo movement back then. Well, there was, but it was more like this:

"Who wants a beer?"

"I do!"

"Me, too!"

Nobody knew anything about all the various subcategories of sexual identity. No one had a clue about people who were bi-coastal or trans-Atlantic or if you were a Jane trapped in the body of a Jim or whatever.[17] And you could pinch a girl's ass without it becoming an issue involving an intervention by a UN peacekeeping team.

If you didn't have to worry about all those things then, well, why do you have to worry about them now? And if you were Doug Ford, you'd have to ask yourself this question: If we didn't know about all this stuff, then how did we turn out to be so well adjusted?

Exactly.

Which is why, when the Ford administration took over, just about the first thing it did was take a look at the sex education curriculum in the province's high schools. There was a lot in the teaching guidelines from the previous Liberal government that was cause for concern. Things like gender identity. Consent. Social media bullying. And a unit on sexting, whatever the hell that is.

The Ford administration wants to be the primary

---

17 Known collectively, more or less by the Ford government, as the BLT people.

source of information and guidance when it comes to shaping young Ontario students' attitudes toward sex, and it sees no reason why it can't be successful in this regard, so long as you don't consider the fact that there are more than a quarter billion porn sites, that roughly 30 percent of the internet is dedicated to pornography, and that millions of people subscribe to all sorts of streaming services, like HBO, which airs *Game of Thrones*, where you can see, especially in the earlier seasons, people going at it like those White Walkers are going to be coming through the gates of Winterfell at any moment.

So, once the Conservative MPPs took office, they immediately embarked on revisions to the sex ed program to make it more traditional and acceptable to the "general population." And the Ford government had no problem with spending a little money to set things right.

Among the initiatives:

- **$3 million for back alleys:** Those dark, narrow, trash-strewn alleyways are where a great many of us learned about the birds and bees. We huddled with friends, perched on the tops of garbage cans, smoking cigarettes we'd stolen from our moms' purses, and shared stories about things we'd heard. There would always be one guy — let's call him Bert — who was only thirteen but said he had already gotten to second base, and he had an older brother who'd gone all the way, so he knew EVERYTHING. We suspected he was full of shit, but it didn't matter, because Bert was a great storyteller.

But we digress.

It was in back alleys, away from the prying eyes of parents, that valuable information could be imparted to the next generation. The Ford government understands that many of the suburbs surrounding Toronto do not have traditional back alleys, so they will be erected[18] in several key locations in the 905 area. In more outlying, rural areas, where building back alleys is problematic, funds will be directed to the construction of tree houses, another key location where young Ontarians can not only learn about sex but see their parents coming from a mile away.

- **$1.3 million for old periodicals:** The education ministry is searching used bookstores and eBay for copies of men's magazines from the 1960s and 1970s. As any male over the age of fifty can tell you, everything one learned about sex was from the pages of these magazines. Hugh Hefner's iconic publication, *Playboy*, is the periodical most eagerly sought,[19] but if not enough copies of that magazine can be obtained, then such titles as *Swank*, *Gallery*, and *Penthouse* will

---

18 Sorry, we just giggled a little there.

19 In particular, the February 1974 issue, with the "Girls of Skiing" pictorial. *Whoosh!*

be considered, just so long as not too many of the pages are stuck together.

One of the side benefits of securing old *Playboy* magazines is they can also be used in the event that schools run out of *Where's Waldo* or the Richard Scarry picture books where you had to find Goldbug. Kids of all ages will love trying to find the *Playboy* bunny logo, which appeared on the cover of every issue often very cleverly hidden, nudge nudge, wink wink.

Considering that there are slightly more than two million students in Ontario, that's a lot of old magazines to be found. There's a concern that when students take them home overnight to complete assignments, they might not be returned.[20] That's why the government has a backup plan of reissuing the Eaton's and Simpsons-Sears catalogues, or at least those pages featuring women's underwear.

- **$100,000 for old paperback copies of *The Godfather***: One of the most memorable scenes in the Mario Puzo novel, where Sonny Corleone has sex with the bridesmaid, is told in such graphic detail that no accompanying pictures are necessary.

- **$430,000 for VCRs:** The adult film industry really took off with the invention of the video cassette recorder in the 1980s. Before this, if you wanted

---

20 Especially if Dad discovers them.

to see a movie where sex was the primary theme, you had to go to some seedy, icky place filled with low-lifes (no, not Queen's Park) and go into a seedier, ickier booth. Or maybe you knew someone with a reel-to-reel projector who could show these things at home, but that was pretty rare. The movies made for VCRs were tamer than the kind of material being shot today, and therefore more palatable for today's concerned parents.

Also, there's a strong moral component to the Ford administration's sex education curriculum, particularly where it relates to the viewing of such material on a VCR. Students will be reminded of one guiding principle:

BE KIND. REWIND.

BALLOT CHOICE CURRENTLY TRENDING IN THE ONTARIO POLLS . . .
None of the Above
GLOBE AND MAIL

CHAPTER FIVE

TRAINING THE NEW MPPS

One of the new shows on Ford TV that I forgot to mention back in Chapter Three is *Planet Doug*, a documentary program that takes an in-depth look at how Queen's Park works. A recent episode regarding the training that goes into being a good MPP for your constituents was especially illuminating.

Let's face it: MPPs come from all walks of life. They might have a professional background. They could be doctors or lawyers. Maybe they were in business, running everything from a major corporation to a small mom-and-pop enterprise. But regardless of where they might have come from, being a member of the provincial legislature is unlike anything they've ever done before.

What's Question Period all about? How does a law come into effect? What are the hiring and firing procedures? How does an MPP protect against conflict of interest? How do you balance your time between your riding and Queen's Park?

There's a pretty steep learning curve.

Premier Ford understands how difficult it can be to get up and running, so he's taken a very personal role in instructing his MPPs in the finer points of governing. In the recent documentary, a camera crew got to tag along to see the premier taking on the role of instructor. The lesson was conducted in a classroom format, with desks that had been taken from a primary classroom in Fenelon Falls.

FORD: Good morning, class!

MPPS: Good morning, Premier Ford!

FORD: *(sounding hurt)* Did we forget something?

(MPPs glance at one another, puzzled)

FORD: Hello? Are our bottoms still in our chairs?

(MPPs, suddenly getting it, are out of their tiny school desks and standing)

FORD: Let's try that again. It's good practice for every time I say anything in Question Period.

(MPPs sit, then stand)

FORD: Faster!

(MPPs sit, then stand, but some get caught in the desks, which are designed for five-year-olds)

FORD: *(wearily)* Okay, let's move on. Okay, you, come up here.

(A male MPP approaches as Ford reaches into his pocket)

FORD: I have a little treat here for you. You like Timbits?

MPP NUMBER ONE: Uh, sure, yeah.

FORD: Okay, so I'm just going to ask you to lean your head back a bit . . . that's good. And I'm going to balance this Timbit on your nose, so all you have to do is hold still until I give the okay and then you can eat it. No using your hands.

MPP NUMBER ONE: Um, okay. But —

FORD: Oh, you dropped it. Let's try again.

MPP NUMBER ONE: Can you use a fresh one? That one hit the floor.

FORD: Five-second rule.

MPP NUMBER ONE: *(sighs)*

FORD: Okay, here we go.

MPP NUMBER ONE: It's a sugary one so that's helping it stick.[21]

---

21 What really works best here is a jam-filled Timbit. The trick is to place the jam insertion point, where there is jam residue, on the bridge of the nose. Give it a little push, and it should hold in place.

FORD: Good. Okay . . . not yet . . . not yet . . . not yet . . . OKAY!

(MPP whips head back, tosses Timbit into the air, and catches it in his mouth)

FORD: Well done! Now, you there, you want to come up?

(A female MPP approaches)

MPP NUMBER TWO: I like Timbits, but I really don't want to —

FORD: Not a problem. Now, you see this big hoop I have here? Let me just hold this up.

MPP NUMBER TWO: Uh . . .

FORD: Now, I just get out my lighter and . . . here we go!

(The hoop erupts into flame, turning into a ring of fire)

FORD: So, I think you know what to do.

MPP NUMBER TWO: Is it okay if I take a run at it?

FORD: Of course!

(She takes a few steps back, then runs toward the hoop. She's about to make the jump when the premier raises it three feet. She hits the brakes.)

FORD: Didn't see that coming, did you?

MPP NUMBER TWO: I gotta be honest. I did not.

FORD: Let's try it again. But keep in mind, you won't be able to just jump through it, you're going to have to leap head first. Kind of *dive*, you know? And just so you're aware, there are points for form.

MPP NUMBER TWO: Got it.

(She backs up again, runs toward the hoop, stretches her arms out in front of her as though diving into a pool, and goes through the hoop)

FORD: Oh, that's excellent. Did everyone see that?

(There is scattered applause from the other MPPs in the class)

FORD: Nice form, well done. I think she deserves a Timbit for that. What does everyone else think?

(More applause)

FORD: Wanna tilt your head back so I can put the Timbit in position?

MPP NUMBER TWO: That sounds great, and honestly, the last thing I'd want to be is a bother, but my hair is on fire.

GLOBE+MAIL GABLE
THIS SHOULD BE INTERESTING.
Toronto City Council

CHAPTER SIX

YOU, TOO, CAN HAVE A NOTWITHSTANDING CLAUSE!

First, a history lesson. Bear with me. If I could animate this, like an episode of *Schoolhouse Rock*, I would.

You've probably heard references to something called "the notwithstanding clause" bandied about over the last year, and maybe you have wanted to ask the guy sitting next to you at the Mars diner on College Street what it is but haven't, because you do not want to look like an idiot. What you don't know is that the guy sitting next to you is also wondering what the hell the notwithstanding clause is but isn't asking you, because he doesn't want to look like an idiot.[22]

So, let me explain.

Back a few years, the federal government came up with something called the Canadian Charter of Rights and Freedoms. Buried in the small print — like all that stuff in a real estate agreement that you know you should read but don't want to, because you're already thinking about how you'll redecorate — was something called the notwithstanding clause. This would give a provincial government the right to basically say "get stuffed" to the charter and the courts and do whatever the hell it wanted, at least for a limited period of time, kind of like if you and your brothers and sisters and your mom had all voted to go to Disney World for March Break, and the hotel and flights had been booked, and then Dad said no, we're all going to Graceland and there wasn't a damn thing you could do about it.

The notwithstanding clause is more or less considered the "nuclear option." If there's something a premier believes he absolutely must do, regardless of what

22 It is also possible that the guy next to you is *not* thinking about the notwithstanding clause and is instead wondering whether the world really needs any more *Star Trek* series or movies, that maybe it's time to let Gene Roddenberry's dream die. And I know this, because that guy is me.

anyone else might think, they can invoke this clause. It's like the "red matter" in just about any J.J. Abrams movie or TV show. When you use it, anything can happen.

When Doug Ford was campaigning back in early 2018, he didn't happen to mention that the most pressing issue facing the people of Ontario — well, right *after* being able to buy beer for a buck — was Toronto City Council. It was too big, he determined. After all, now that he was no longer actually part of it, what kind of real contribution could it be expected to make?

So, right in the midst of the fall municipal election — candidates had all declared, put up their signs, and were in the middle of knocking on doors — Premier Ford introduced the Better Local Government Act[23] that would cut the number of council seats from forty-seven to twenty-five. This is like having a party with a bunch of your buds, ordering ten pizzas with double cheese, and then your last friend arrives late and says he's lactose intolerant.

The courts dismissed injunctions to try to stop Ford from doing this. Had they not, he was ready to use the notwithstanding clause to get his way, and his supporters were totally on board. (Whenever you are

---

23 The Ford government's rumoured upcoming legislation to slash mental health program funding is to be called A Smile Is Just a Frown Turned Upside Down Act.

sticking it to Toronto, pretty much everyone outside of Toronto is on board.)

I know what you're thinking. What if *I* had that kind of power? What if *I* could have my very own notwithstanding clause? What if *I* could have a bunch of them?

Well, guess what? Now you can!

With every $100 donation to the Progressive Conservative Party of Ontario, you will receive one Notwithstanding Card. It's the size of a business card and fits easily in your wallet.

Let's say you're in the drive-through line at your local Tim Hortons. There are at least a dozen cars in front of you. You need that morning double-double very badly. Not only that, it's going to take so long to get through this line that you're going to be late for work.

What are you to do?[24]

Simple!

You get out of your car and flash your Notwithstanding Card to every motorist ahead of you. Get to the car next in line to be served, tap on the window, and display that card right in front of the driver's nose. They

---

24 One thing you are definitely NOT going to do is park your fucking car and just walk into the fucking Tim Hortons and get your fucking coffee and get back in your fucking car in a mere fraction of the fucking time it would have taken to go through the fucking drive-through.

will understand that the Notwithstanding Card entitles the bearer to flout all social conventions.

Then you go back to your car, get out of line, drive past the cars ahead of you — and cut in. Is that awesome or what?

Or let's say you're zipping along Highway 407, the toll highway that runs across the top of Toronto. It's wide open, hardly a car to be seen, which is hard to figure, considering that all you need to travel the 407 is a transponder, a legible licence plate, and a seven-figure income.

Given that you have the highway to yourself, you decide to open it up a bit. Your foot presses down hard on the accelerator. Before you know it, you're doing 200 kilometres per hour! *Whee!!!!!*

And that's when you hear the siren. There, in your rear-view mirror, is an Ontario Provincial Police cruiser, lights flashing.

So, you pull over. The officer approaches.

"Licence and registration," the officer says, "and a Notwithstanding Card, if you possess one."

It just so happens you do! Off you go, without a ticket. Not even a warning! Is this a great province or what?

A word of caution, however. With great power comes great responsibility. Do not let your Notwithstanding Card fall into the wrong hands. It's worse than losing a fully loaded Presto card. Guard yours carefully.

Case in point:

On March 12, 2019, in Millbrook, Ontario, long-time PC supporter Bud Budley could not find his Notwithstanding Cards. He had made a $1,000 donation to the party and had been sent ten cards, and he had used only one of them, the night before, when his spouse had said she had a headache.

Where were the rest of them?

And then his wife appeared at the top of the stairs, fanning the cards in her hand.

"Looking for these?" she asked.

Last we heard, Bud was still working on building an addition onto their house all by himself, and his wife was still in the Bahamas.

hydro One
Executive
Salaries
VOTERS
GLOBE+MAIL

CHAPTER SEVEN

THE TAKING OF PELHAM TTC

When considering Doug Ford's moves to take over the Toronto Transit Commission, to literally steal the subway system away from the city, one's mind wanders back to 1974, when a movie called *The Taking of Pelham One Two Three* was released.[25]

In the film, Robert Shaw, best remembered as Quint from *Jaws*, plays the head of a group of terrorists who seize a New York City subway car and threaten to kill the passengers if the city does not pay a ransom of $1 million. Of course, it's somewhat ridiculous to compare

---

25 There was a remake in 2009, starring Denzel Washington, and the less said about that, the better.

this to what Doug Ford and his people are proposing. In the movie, Shaw and his partners are well organized and know what they're doing.

Over the years, Toronto and its various mayors and councillors have struggled with how to improve the transit system and spent roughly $12.2 billion working up various proposals.[26] But more recently, they have settled on some basic needs, including a so-called relief line that would add some stops in the city's southeast downtown core and relieve pressure on the Yonge and Bloor lines. Ford had decreed that this very local, downtown Toronto line will be called, and I am not making this up, the "Ontario" line, which is a bit like if your mom buys you a car, but only on the condition that it has a personalized licence plate that reads "MY SNOOKUMS."

Now that the city has more or less figured out what it needs to do, the Ford government has stepped in and said all those plans are stupid, the city doesn't know what it's doing, that they need to go back to the drawing board, and start all over again.

Toronto Mayor John Tory, standing up for the people of his city who do not like to be pushed around by higher levels of government, especially when those higher levels of government are led by someone they

---

26 I just made that number up. For all I know, that's way too low.

believe has the IQ of a six-pack, responded forcefully by saying, "Yes, well, maybe you're right, I don't know, I guess we could listen to what you have to say, there's no harm in that, I suppose."

Like his late brother, who championed subways over any other kind of transit mode because he was always getting stuck behind streetcars in his Escalade, Premier Ford doesn't have much time for surface routes.

"We're going to build, build, build subways, subways, subways," Ford said, but not before the Ministry of Health commits $1 million to help people with stuttering problems.

The Ford administration has laid out a transit plan it believes is nothing short of brilliant. Some of the highlights:

- Make the north-south Yonge subway line an east-west line, and make the east-west Bloor subway line a north-south line. This means, in all likelihood, that wherever you might want to go, you're probably already there. Realigning these two transit lines will allow passengers to go madly off in all directions.[27]

- Turn all Subway sandwich shops into transit stops. They're already all over the place, and we don't have to spend any extra money on signage.

---

27 Dear S.L.: The cheque's in the mail.

- No longer require motorists to stop from driving along the inside lane when the streetcar doors open. Dodging between moving vehicles as they step off the streetcar will make riders more "resilient."[28]

- Build a monorail, but with a difference! Put it underground! Years ago, Doug Ford and his brother pitched the idea of a monorail for Toronto, but now that the push is on for subways, why not combine the two transportation modes? You start by building a subway tunnel, but just make it deeper so there's enough room under the train for hot dog stands. If this works, the government is going to revolutionize airplane travel by building runways throughout the city, thereby enabling 747s to move people all over the place without actually taking off.

(There is, of course, no truth to the rumour Doug Ford is mucking about with Toronto's transit plans merely to delay them, so that all that spending won't have to happen on his watch.)

But the most interesting proposal from the provincial government is also the most ambitious — possibly the most grandiose project in the history of public transit anywhere in the world.

The Ford government will soon embark on a northward

---

28 See class-size argument in the schools chapter.

extension of the Yonge subway line (soon to be the Bloor line, but you get the idea) that will start at North York Centre and go for 199 kilometres.

The line will run parallel to Highway 400 north to Barrie, then take a slight jog to the east and continue northward alongside Highway 11, past Bracebridge, through the Muskoka lakes tourism region, finally reaching its end point in Port Sydney, where Highway 11 intersects with Highway 141.

Given that the entire line will be underground, it will in no way disturb the pristine, majestic beauty of the Muskoka landscape, except during the construction period, which is expected to take twenty years and destroy the natural habitat of every single Ontario species of wildlife.

There will be no stops between North York and Port Sydney. This is a direct, non-stop ride, and it will consist of a single track instead of two. And rather than run a subway train of several cars, there will be just one car, and it will go up on Friday evenings and come back on Sunday nights.

And before anyone starts making wild accusations, it's pure coincidence that Port Sydney is where the Ford family has its cottage.

Responding to suggestions that this line serves no one but the Ford family, the premier reacted angrily: "That is an absolutely outrageous statement. I can't believe the opposition would stoop to such baseless accusations. But I will have to admit, weekend traffic is a bitch on the 400, and short of using my new, special premier's Batcopter, this is going to be the fastest way to get up there."

OSHAWA
GM
GLOBE+MAIL

CHAPTER EIGHT

HAVE YOU DRIVEN A FORD VAN LATELY?

When you're a provincial premier, you expect to be driven around on official business in something better than a Kia, right?

So, it was no surprise that when Doug Ford got the top job, he wanted an awesome ride. The previous premier, Kathleen Wynne, was chauffeured around in a big, black Chevy Suburban, which is not a bad car but lacks the kind of flash that a real premier with an ego the size of the CN Tower demands.

Premier Ford wanted a van. Not just any van, but a van outfitted with a leather sofa, a Blu-ray player, a big-screen TV, a mini-fridge, a bowling alley, a roller coaster, a fishing pond, and a barbecue. What he was looking for was going to cost about $50,000, not counting the cost of the actual van. And he wanted the money that he would need to customize his ride to be, according to one Ontario Provincial Police official, "off the books."

Well, that just makes sense. If you are a superhero — and if anyone is a superhero, it would have to be the premier of the country's largest province — you have to be discreet about your wheels.

Isn't this exactly what Bruce Wayne did? When he needed a special vehicle for fighting crime, he went to Lucius Fox, the business manager at Wayne Enterprises, otherwise known as WayneCorp., who showed him the little toy they had down in the basement that the R&D department had been working on. *Totally off the books.*

As a matter of fact, a Batmobile was one of the first vehicles considered for the premier, but there were a number of issues. Which Batmobile? The one from the old TV show, adapted from a Lincoln Futura? The one from the Tim Burton–directed movies that looked like an enormous schlong with fins? The militaristic Tumbler from the Christopher Nolan films?

Regardless of which Batmobile was chosen, space was an issue. The most any of these cars could carry was two people. What if the premier wanted to bring along campaign strategists? Advisers? Someone to throw steaks on the barbecue?

And if he were in a Batmobile, would Premier Ford be expected to wear a cape? Sources say he was okay with that, but he wasn't crazy about wearing the mask all the time because it would make his face all sweaty.

So, the Batmobile idea was abandoned. But several proposals remain on the drawing board for a vehicle suitable for someone of Doug Ford's stature. Automotive engineers are ready to build one, or even all, of the following:

- The Mystery Machine, the van used by Velma and Scooby and Shaggy in the *Scooby-Doo* cartoon series. When the premier was shown some initial sketches, he reportedly said, "Ri rike it!" The original van was fitted with computers, a table and chairs, ropes and lanterns, and a ladder in case they had to scale the perimeter wall of some haunted house late at night. The only negative could be the big flower decals on the side, which have a "hippie" connotation and might even lead people to think it was a "weed delivery vehicle."[29]

- A 1983 GMC van decorated to look just like the vehicle from *The A-Team*. If it was good enough for George Peppard and Mr. T, surely it would be good enough for Doug Ford. The only concern raised by aides is what people will think the "A" stands for.

---

29 There was a time when this might have been ideal.

- A DeLorean, customized to look like the one used in the *Back to the Future* movies, is high on the list of possible vehicles, even though it does offer limited interior room. The upside is it will allow Doug Ford to take Ontarians back to a time when men were men, women were women, and you could take a whiz off the end of the dock without having every member of the Green Party stepping out of the woods and pointing the finger of shame.

- The Oscar Mayer Wienermobile, designed by the Oscar Mayer company in the United States to publicize its hot dogs. It looks like an enormous wiener on wheels, which would seem to have a lot going for it as ride for the premier. It's got the common touch — it's not like Doug Ford would be caught dead in a Kale-mobile — and would basically neuter protesters' attempts to deface the premier's car with mustard, ketchup, or other condiments.[30]

- A Transformers vehicle. A provincial premier's van modelled after Bumblebee, Megatron, Optimus Prime, Devastator, or any of the other characters from the

---

30 True story: In 2009, in Wisconsin, the driver of a Wienermobile, while attempting to turn around in a dead-end street, mistakenly hit the gas instead of the brake and rammed the vehicle into a house. Next time you update your house insurance policy, you might want to ask whether you're covered for catastrophic wiener incidents.

popular TV and movie franchise that morph from ordinary cars and trucks into monstrous robots would be a hit with the kids, to be sure. Any time word gets out that Doug Ford is coming to town in his Transformer, little ones will literally drag their parents to the event. But the real upside is any time the premier encounters a protest at what is supposed to be a campaign rally, all he has to do is push a button to turn his ride into a towering, fire-breathing metal monster and stomp his naysayers into street pizza.

L'état, C'est Moi
NOTE... THE FRENCH LANGUAGE IN ONTARIO!
OPP Chief Appointed by Cabinet
GLOBE+MAIL

CHAPTER NINE

"JE SUIS DOESN'T GIVE A SHIT"

No sooner had Doug Ford become premier than he made a bold move to make the French-speaking residents of Ontario as "resilient" as he planned to make the province's student population. (More about that in the following chapter.)

The Ministry of Francophone Affairs was eliminated.

The position of the French language services commissioner was axed.

Plans by the previous administration to establish the province's first French-language university were thrown into the Dumpster.

These moves, for reasons that seemed to baffle the Ford government, did not go over well in communities where French is widely spoken. In fact, Ford and most of his fellow Conservatives seemed to be unaware that there are more than 620,000 Franco-Ontarians. This became evident during Ford's bid for the Progressive Conservative leadership, when he spoke about the need to stay on good terms with all those French-speaking Quebecers.

French-speaking Ontarians responded with "Nous sommes ici!" Or, "We're over here!"

One of those Ontarians just happened to be one of Ford's own MPPs, Amanda Simard, from the riding of Glengarry-Prescott-Russell, which the premier kept thinking was called Glengarry Glen Ross, which contains one of his all-time favourite movie lines.[31]

When Simard found herself unable to justify these decisions to her own constituents, she resigned as a Progressive Conservative and decided to sit as an independent, which meant that she would no longer be able to have her voice heard in the Conservative caucus, the premier would not care how she felt on any issue, and he would not be the slightest bit interested in any idea she might want to put forward. In other words, she would continue to be treated exactly the same as all the other backbench MPPs who had *not* left the PC party.

---

31 "ABC. Always Be Conservative."

It was hard to fault Ford for not knowing there were any French-speaking people in Ontario. When you've grown up in Etobicoke, about the only French you were exposed to was on a cereal box or on a restaurant breakfast menu that offered French toast. You might have had a French class or two in high school, but that was about it. If you weren't planning to take a trip to Montreal or Quebec City, you could pretty much get along without ever having to use the word "fenêtre."

When the backlash to these decisions didn't seem to be going away, Ford opted to reinstate the commissioner position, although the French university proposal stayed dead. He gave any French-language responsibilities to Caroline Mulroney, since she didn't have much else to do.

In a heartfelt statement intended to put these issues behind him, Ford said, "Je suis tres sorry for le boo boo."

Fearing that might not be enough to show how sincere he was about his love for French-speaking Ontarians, he did an entire episode on Ford TV listing all the French things that he absolutely loves:

- French fries
- French dressing
- French bread
- French kissing (within a loving, committed relationship, of course)

— French bulldogs (oh my God, they are just adorable)

— French press coffee

— French horn

— French vanilla

If that doesn't win all those Franco-Ontarians back into the PC fold, what would?

NEW IMPROVED HIGH SCHOOL CLASS SIZES
FURTHERMORE, THIS WILL PROVIDE INVALUABLE EXPERIENCE TO THOSE STUDENTS PREPARING FOR CAREERS IN THE SARDINE INDUSTRY.
Ontario Ministry of Education
GLOBE+MAIL

CHAPTER TEN

THE SCHOOLS: MAKE ONTARIO RESILIENT AGAIN

If it's one thing Progressive Conservative governments like to have fun with, it's schools. Back when Mike Harris was premier, he had an education minister by the name of John Snobelen, and Snobelen was caught on video saying that the best thing you could do with the educational system was "create a crisis" in it.

Snobelen and the other education ministers who succeeded him in that administration were immensely successful in this regard. They didn't just create one crisis. They created a slew of them. Ontario had education crises coming out of its ass.

It was a glorious time.

Clearly inspired by the PCs who had come before him, Premier Ford is eager to put his stamp on the province's schools, and not just in the area of sex education, which we covered in an earlier chapter. If you skipped it, we'll wait.

Perhaps the most obvious change that Ford is implementing is in the area of average class size. When his former education minister, Lisa Thompson, appeared on CBC Radio's *Metro Morning* in March 2019, she came up with the most brilliant reason ever to increase the number of kids in Ontario classrooms.

She said that once kids move on to post-secondary institutions, they were going to encounter very large class sizes, so in an effort to make Ontario students more "resilient," it made sense to increase, at the high school level, the average number of students any given teacher must deal with.[32] In other words, get used to it. Not only would this make students more resilient, it would make teachers more resilient, too.

But why stop at class size? There are many other ways to give students a taste of what awaits them in the big, bad world. Let's make them as resilient as possible

---

32 Basically, this: In a bid to prepare Ontario's kids for getting fucked over on a daily basis when they enter the real world, the province will start fucking them over while they're still in school.

— and see if we can't cut some money out of the education budget at the same time.

For example, is it ever too early to teach a kid how to operate and maintain a boiler? If you start teaching children some engineering basics in, say, Grade 3, by the time they're in Grade 5 they should be able to look after the school's heating system. Sure, there's a bit of blood, sweat, and tears involved, but isn't that what building resilience is all about?

And the added bonus? Think how much money you can save when you fire all the janitors whose job it was to do this.

What about school buses? Shouldn't students accept responsibility, as early as possible, for getting themselves to school and home again? Sure, the legal driving age is sixteen, but there's no reason why the Ford government couldn't make an exception in this case. As soon as kids are able to reach the pedals and see over the steering wheel, why not put them in the driver's seat? In fact, why wait that long? If you have one kid working the pedals, and another up top working the wheel, what better way to teach teamwork and communication skills?

Kid One: *There's a cow in the road! Hit the brakes! Hit the brakes!*

Kid Two: *Why should I do all the work? Steer around it, asshole!*

And, once again, we have the added bonus of firing all the school bus drivers. The potential savings to taxpayers are enormous.

What about Pizza Day? Plenty of schools organize pizza days, particularly in the lower grades. These days are often used as fundraisers to buy supplies or hold special activities, like field days. Some kids *live* for Pizza Days. They mark them on their calendars. Kids who are inclined to feign illness *never* get sick on a Pizza Day.

A Pizza Day can be a terrific way to teach resilience. It's simple. Take the number of kids who are expecting to get a slice of pizza, then reduce the number of slices by 20 percent. So if there are twenty kids, make sure you have only sixteen slices. See what happens. This makes for an excellent "survival of the fittest" lesson.

Finally, let's take a long, hard look at class outings.

The Ford government is preparing a new instructional handbook for teachers. It's called "Taking Your Kids to Ripley's Aquarium," and outlines, in detail, how to get the students ready.

Needless to say, students will be pretty excited about going to Ripley's Aquarium, one of the top tourist attractions in Toronto. It'll be great fun and a terrific learning experience.

The handbook lays out several days of lesson plans leading up to the day of the excursion. There are units on various sea creatures, underwater plant life, how an aquarium is built, and how the fish are looked after.

When the teacher reaches the end of the handbook, for the very last lesson, you can bet she'll be just as amazed as the students. Why?

Because there is no trip! There was never *going* to be a trip! The whole exercise was a trick!

What better way to prepare kids for the world — to build resilience — than to introduce them to two basic fundamentals of life:

1. It's full of disappointment.
2. Even the people you think you can trust will lie their asses off to you.

And, as if you didn't already know, the money the province has saved by not arranging transportation to the aquarium or buying the kids tickets will find its way, by way of a tax cut, into the pocket of some Bay Street stock trader so he can order the chilled seafood tower at the Shore Club.

TEACHER PROTESTS

Doug Ford, from the beginning, has warned the province's teacher unions that they better not strike over anything he wants to do to the education system. Don't even think about it. After all, he points out, teachers have got it pretty easy. They've got all summer off, plus all the other holidays.[33] (It should be pointed out that the five-month 2019 summer recess Doug Ford gave himself made the teachers look like total amateurs.)

The truth is many teachers are trying to finagle their way out of the profession so they can get into a job with even better perks. They would like a job where you get paid twice as much, where you get nearly three months off in the winter, where you get a housing allowance, and where you can expense all your gas and travel costs.

That job, of course, is Member of Provincial Parliament.

BULLYING POLICIES

For a long time now, Ontario schools have been embracing anti-bullying policies. They've been teaching kids strategies for how to deal with other kids who bully them and also have tried to drive home the message that being a bully is a very, very bad thing.

Well, you can kiss those lessons goodbye.

It's a whole new ball game. Unless you've been living on Neptune for the last few years, you'll have noticed that the world has gotten a whole lot tougher, and a

---

33 I've said it before and I'll say it again: If it was turned around, and they taught two months of the year and had the other ten off, I still wouldn't want to be a teacher.

whole lot meaner, and the general public is eating it up like rocky road ice cream. Check out a political rally these days, north or south of the border. You could be forgiven for thinking you had stumbled into an arena featuring staged fights with costumed wrestlers.

Political leaders are often looked up to as role models. And the role models that children have today are sending out one message loud and clear: "I don't give a rat's ass about your precious feelings, you four-eyed, pencil-necked, butt-sniffing loser."

This is the world we have to prepare our kids for, and let's face it, if you've got a choice between being the one who holds the kid's head in the toilet while you flush it, or the kid who's getting flushed, who are you going to pick?

If you're looking for a role model in this new world, you could do a lot worse than Doug Ford. Just ask any members of his caucus who have dared to speak out against him. They've been mocked and humiliated and, in some cases, kicked out. When Doug Ford thought he wasn't going to get his way when it came to decimating Toronto City Council, he threatened to use the notwithstanding clause, the ultimate political bullying tool. Ditto on subways.[34] What Doug wants, Doug gets.

---

34 If you look in the dictionary under "bullying victim," you will find a picture of Toronto mayor John Tory, cowering.

But as is the case with any new curriculum, it must be carefully crafted, depending on the grade. The education ministry is setting out three basic levels of bullying instruction:

- **Primary:** Children in kindergarten through to Grade 6 will learn the basics. Simple taunting: "I know you are but what am I?", tripping, pulling down a victim's pants and running away, dipping a girl's pigtails into the inkwell on your desk.[35]

- **Grades 7 and 8:** By now, most kids have mastered their computer skills, know how to surf the net, and are active on social media. This is the best time to introduce students to bullying tactics that require no actual physical contact or face-to-face unpleasantness. Some of the terms that will be discussed include "piling on," "public shaming," and "mob mentality."

- **High School:** Once students get to Grade 9, they're ready to incorporate all the bullying methods they've learned up to now and to add a few new ones. This is when you can combine social media threats with actual physical intimidation. For example, a student could send a text to someone that reads "nxt time i c u im gonna rearrange ur ugly face," and then, the

---

35 They still have those, right?

following day, do exactly that. And a lot of the old standbys still work: locking a kid in his locker, Swirling 101 (see "head in toilet" paragraph above), a nipple-twister in the boys' change room.

The new curriculum can pretty much be summed up with an ever-so-slightly altered quote by somebody else from somewhere, sometime in the past:

"Do unto others before they have a chance to do it unto you."

Political Bombast Sign Storage Depot
APPARENTLY THEY USED TO MAKE CARS AND STUFF HERE.
GM
Welcome To
ONTARIO
OPEN FOR BUSINESS
GLOBE&MAIL

CHAPTER ELEVEN

WAITING FOR A SIGN . . .

Across the globe, presidents and kings and queens and prime ministers had been waiting . . . for a sign.

Titans of industry rose each day and looked skyward, as though the answer might be found in the heavens, that some kind of sign might be hidden in the clouds.

They all studied economic forecasts, watched the twenty-four-hour news stations, scanned every financial website for the tiniest of clues to what might be coming. No method of trying to predict the world economy was discounted. There were reports that some of the heads of the biggest corporations in the world tracked sunspots, read tea leaves. Leaders of nations quietly consulted astrologists, even psychics, looking for a sign of what the future might hold.

In Australia:

Prime Minister: G'day, my senior adviser. Anything to report? Have you seen any . . . sign?

Adviser: Nothing, I'm afraid.

In Germany:

BMW CEO: Day after day, I wait for a sign. Tell me something is coming!

BMW Head of Sales: We have been searching everywhere, but I am sorry to say, the sign we are waiting for has not materialized.

But then, one day, there was a miracle.

Word began to spread that the sign everyone had been waiting for — no, *praying* for — had been seen.

It had appeared in what seemed the most unlikely of places: Sarnia, Ontario, Canada. It had been spotted along the side of the road as one drove into the country from the United States.

The sign read:

WELCOME TO ONTARIO:
OPEN FOR BUSINESS

The sign was big. It was on a billboard. The letters were very tall. It was everything anyone could want in a sign.

Across the globe there was jubilation! At long last, the sign they had been waiting for!

"Oh, this is wondrous!" shouted workers in the streets of Tokyo.

Great cries of joy erupted on Wall Street. "We knew this day would come!" traders shouted, tears in their eyes.

Even as far away as Singapore, there were fireworks.

This sign, this "Welcome to Ontario: Open for Business," was a total game-changer. The world's movers and shakers now knew what to do.

They would invest in Ontario. How could they not? The sign was compelling. It was persuasive.

As everyone knows, in the days before the appearance of the sign — what were known as the "dark days" in Ontario — there was no business. Factories lay dormant. Storefronts were papered over. Tumbleweeds blew through Bay Street in Toronto. Wolf packs roamed the Byward Market in Ottawa. Orphaned children searched empty homes in Peterborough, looking for scraps of food. Cars were left abandoned on the sides of Highways 400 and 401 as their drivers and passengers wandered into the woods in search of edible berries. Some were forced to kill wild animals with their bare hands to survive.

But the sign went up, and everything changed.

The sun came out. The clouds cleared. The rivers receded.

Once again, Ontario was open for business.

Who could have predicted that this was all it would take? But we have come to appreciate, throughout history, the power of signs. That star in the night sky that led those wise men to Bethlehem. When that meteor struck Earth millions of years ago, the dinosaurs got the message that their days were numbered. Great cinema is filled with signs. When Richard Dreyfuss, in *Close Encounters of the Third Kind*, starts sculpting Devil's Tower out of his mashed potatoes, it's a sign that contact with aliens is imminent.

But those all pale in comparison to the one that greeted folks driving into Canada at Sarnia.

At that point, Ontarians began to emerge from the woods where they had sought shelter and, in some cases, resorted to cannibalism to survive. The wolf packs disappeared. The tumbleweeds blew away. People returned to their homes, some horrified to find that they had not thought to turn back the thermostat before leaving.

Factories resumed production as investors from Mexico to Malaysia were caught up in the sign's magical spell and invested billions in the province's economy. There was prosperity unlike anything anyone had ever seen, except for maybe the 2,500 jobs lost at the GM plant in Oshawa, or the 1,500 jobs cut at the Fiat Chrysler plant in Windsor, or the therapists fired from autism clinics, or the number of teaching positions that would be lost as larger class sizes were imposed.

But hey, there was pretty much universal agreement that the sign was a work of genius.

What brilliant mind was behind all this? What great lord-like presence oversaw the realization of this sign?

It was . . . *Doug*.

And is it just a coincidence that "Doug" spelled backwards is "Guod?"

We don't think so.

REMEMBER WHEN IT WAS JUST COMPULSORY STICKERS?
NO CARBON TAX

CHAPTER TWELVE

ARE YOU GETTING ENOUGH CARBON FIBRE IN YOUR DIET?

To get an idea of how committed Doug Ford is to reducing the tax burden on Ontarians, it's helpful to look at the various taxes we pay, each and every day, and see where the premier stands on eliminating them.

The chart on the next page should help:

Taxes Doug Ford Rarely Mentions	Taxes That Drive Doug Ford Apeshit
— property tax	— carbon tax
— import tax	
— export tax	
— land transfer tax	
— payroll tax	
— Ontario health premium	
— race tracks tax	
— corporate tax	
— tobacco tax	
— estate administration tax	
— goods and services tax	
— beer and wine tax	
— mining tax	
— corporate tax	
— non-resident speculation tax	
— international fuel tax agreement	

Now, let's review. On the left side of the chart are taxes Ontarians already pay. Some are federal, some provincial, some municipal. Some are levied against individuals while others are levied against businesses. On the right side of the chart is a new tax brought in by the federal government to reduce greenhouse-gas emissions, which many scientists say are linked to a thinning of the ozone layer and climate change and global warming and rising oceans and melting polar ice caps. Those kinds of things. The idea is if Canadians start using everything from cars to light bulbs that consume less energy and create fewer pollutants, they won't have to pay the carbon tax, and the world will become a better, more liveable place.

Have you ever heard anything more stupid in your life? Do you remember how cold it got last year? Remember that day last January when you talked your little brother into putting his tongue on the parking meter pole, and he's still there?

The carbon tax bothers Doug Ford more than any other tax because it is based on the mythical problem of man-made climate change. If the good Lord had not intended for us to live in the manner to which we have become accustomed, He wouldn't have created fuel injection.

You might as well bring in an alien invasion tax that would raise funds to repel Martians when (not *if* and when, just when) they attack Ontario. (And if Martians *did* attack Earth, you can be sure the last place they would invade is Ontario. They would attack France, because the bread there is to die for.)

Everyone knows that if you put one hundred climate scientists into a room, ninety-nine of them are going to say climate change is really happening, and that the human race is responsible. But there will be one scientist who'll say that's a bunch of hogwash. Who are you going to believe?

Stupid question. You're going to believe that guy who says man-made climate change is a bunch of hooey, because then you can still fill up your gas-guzzling Tahoe SUV with relatively inexpensive unleaded. Similarly, if you went to a hundred doctors and ninety-nine of them told you to lose weight or you'll die, and just one doctor told you to just keep on doing what you're doing, you'd listen to that guy because you really don't want to give up your Cheez Doodles.

All of which explains why one of the first things Doug Ford did when he became premier, in addition to getting rid of a provincial children's advocate[36] and a French language services commissioner, was fire the environmental commissioner. The last thing you need when you're trying to boost the economy is someone rapping at your window saying, "You're killing people!" It's annoying.

The Ford administration conducted wide-ranging surveys to gauge Ontarians' reactions to the carbon issue. Its findings:

---

36 This just made sense. Premier Ford got rid of the child advocate, arguing that if you're going to work for the provincial government, you should at least be eighteen.

- Some expressed concern about possible tooth decay.
- Bloating and gas were an issue for others.
- Sometimes it fizzes up and makes your nose feel funny.

It was at this point the province realized the firm conducting the survey had asked Ontarians how they felt about carbonated beverages.

What the government believed it really needed was one compelling reason for voters to get behind opposition to the carbon tax, beyond the most obvious one of increased gas prices. After all, that's been happening *forever*. And once they had a reason they believed would really connect with the public, they could then come up with evidence to support it. Which is not difficult, if you still have that one scientist out of a hundred on your payroll.

The Ford administration came up with this:

The carbon tax is a leading cause of erectile dysfunction.

And why is that?

Well, carbon in the air increases blood flow.[37] If a

---

37 Go ahead. File a Freedom of Information request to get this study. But you're not allowed to say that you're asking for a friend.

carbon tax aims to reduce the level of carbon, and you breathe in less of it, well, do we really have to connect the dots for you on this one?

Now, you may be saying, "Oh, come on." You may be saying, "That's the most ridiculous thing I've ever heard in my life." You may be saying, "There's no real, reliable data to support this conclusion."

Maybe.

But do you want to take that chance?

THERE *IS* A CLIMATE CHANGE PLAN

All that you've read so far in this chapter is not to suggest that the Ontario government is not committing funds to the climate change issue.

Nothing could be further from the truth.

The government is committed to spending thousands of dollars on anti–carbon tax stickers for gas station owners to display prominently on their pumps.

But then the Ford administration decided to print up a few more stickers and use them even more efficiently. These stickers will be sent to various ministry offices throughout the province with instructions that they be used whenever any government staffer shows any inclination whatsoever to utter the words "climate change." If it appears something like that is going to happen, several stickers will be firmly affixed over the staffer's mouth until they agree to talk about something else, like whether the Leafs can finally get it together this year.

If the staffer is considering typing the words "climate change" on social media, perhaps, or even in an email to a co-worker or, God forbid, a member of the media, stickers are to be wrapped securely around the individual's fingers, thereby making it impossible to type without making egregious, discrediting typos.

Carbon Tax
OTHER THAN THAT, WHAT'S YOUR STRATEGY?
ONT.
GLOBE+MAIL GABLE

CHAPTER THIRTEEN

THE FORD GOVERNMENT'S AUTISM PLAN: WALK IT OFF! THE FORD GOVERNMENT'S HEALTH CARE PLAN: DITTO

Here's what Lisa MacLeod told folks in her riding of Nepean, in a fundraising email, back during the 2018 provincial election campaign, with regard to therapy programs for children with autism:

> . . . there are 23,000 families on a waiting list right now.
>
> They're waiting for help.
>
> These families are struggling.
>
> They've got children with autism, and they're not getting help.
>
> My job is to make sure the children on the wait list get off the wait list.
>
> So their parents get the help they need.

Our plan means every family will get funding — directly.

We're not going to keep funnelling the money through bad bureaucracy.

We're not going to keep those kids on a waiting list.

Our critics are focused on industry insiders.

We're focused on helping the kids.

. . . I hope you're with us on this.

Pretty awesome, huh?

If you have a child with autism, you had to feel encouraged that once Lisa was in charge, there'd be someone at Queen's Park fighting on your behalf. And lo and behold, after Lisa was made the minister of community and social services, she immediately had a meeting with the parents and associations who are champions for autistic children and told them if they didn't support the government's plan, they'd be facing "four long years."

The Ford government had worked out a formula to provide therapy to children with autism based on the child's age and the family's income. But critics said what the government was not considering was a child's individual needs. There was even an internal report, conducted by the government itself, that concluded the Ford administration deliberately spread misinformation about its proposed changes to the autism program to justify radical cost-cutting moves.[38]

What those naysayers — inside and outside the government — were not taking into account was that with this issue, more than any other, the Ford government was adopting a faith-based approach.

It was a "loaves and fishes" solution.

If there are 23,000 families waiting to get help for an autistic family member, and only 8,000 are currently receiving assistance, you rearrange — but do not add to — your resources so that all 31,000 can get the same level of service. This way, everyone will be treated equally shitty.[39]

It makes perfect sense, if you're Doug Ford.

While a linear graphic is not that helpful to explain the spectrum of autism, given that it is a complex condition that does not lend itself to a simple scale, a more or less straightforward graph can help explain various spectrums as they relate to the Ford government.

For example, here's where the current provincial government lands on various issues on a so-called spectrum.

---

38 This brings to mind that scary movie line: "The critics' calls are coming from inside the house!"

39 Also known as "doing less for more."

Ford Government's "What We REALLY Give a Rat's Ass About" Spectrum

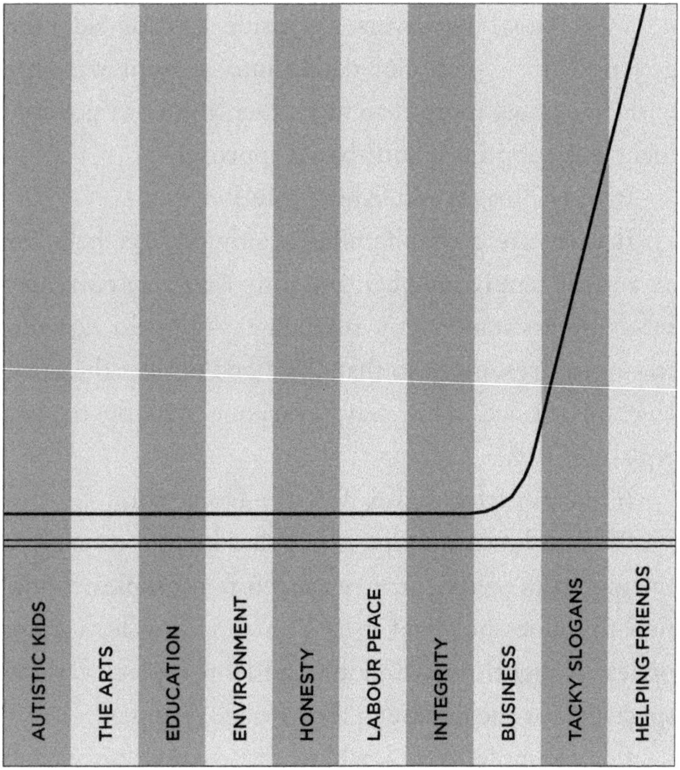

AND THE BROADER HEALTH CARE PICTURE?

There's been a lot of moaning and griping about the Ford government's cut to health care, but if the complainers would only take a minute to look at what the premier is proposing, maybe they'd shut their clanging manholes.

Now that the Ministry of Health has been folded into the newly created Ministry of Beer,[40] there's an opportunity for an entirely new approach to the delivery of health care services.

It's called **Tailgate Medicine**.

Now, when the Ford government said it was making tailgating legal, there was some initial confusion. "You mean we can now ride on people's bumpers with impunity?" That was just stupid. Have you *been* on the 401 lately? Tailgating has clearly been legal in Ontario since cars have had tires.[41]

What the government was making legal was the practice of hosting an alcohol-laced party from the back of your car — tailgating referring, of course, to the back end of a station wagon — in parking lots at sporting events and other venues. But you don't need an actual tailgate. If you want to hold your party out of the trunk of your dinky little Kia sedan, go right ahead and get blasted.

But if you can hold a booze-up just about anywhere, why not apply the same principle to health care? Sure, maybe your local health unit has closed down, and your

---

40 You heard about that, right? It was in the budget. You didn't get the memo?

41 Also, poking along at 70 kilometres per hour in the left lane. Don't. Get. Me. Started.

hospital has half the nurses it used to, but it's very likely that right now, in your own neighbourhood, a tailgate clinic is driving around, just looking for a little action.

Wave one down the way you might a taxi or order it up like an Uber.[42] Tell the driver what ails you and he'll see what he's got in the back to help out. A Pabst Blue Ribbon? Some REACTINE, maybe?

If you've got something more serious, keep your eye out for a **Tailgate Utility Mobile Operating Room (TUMOR)**. You can spot these easily: they're the ones with the back seats already folded down.

And if you're looking for the best in anaesthesia, you could do worse than Absolut Citron.

---

42 There will be a basic Tailgate Party app, and if you're looking for medical attention, just tap on the Suture icon.

Water Found On Mars!!!
HOW DO WE GET TO MARS?
GABLE GLOBE AND MAIL

CHAPTER FOURTEEN

LIBRARIES AND TREES: WHAT HAVE THEY DONE FOR YOU LATELY?

Doug Ford has adopted a "take no prisoners" attitude where libraries and trees are concerned. While his contempt for both is easy to understand — trees have been getting a free ride for a long time now and as for libraries, I mean, come on — what's not as well understood is how the premier developed such strong feelings on these two issues.

Rumour has it that it all goes back to a traumatic event during the premier's childhood.

Doug and his brother Rob had a tree house in the backyard of their Etobicoke home. It made a great hangout. They would climb up there with snacks and pop and comic books and have just the best time.

One day, Doug was up in the tree house with a buddy who'd climbed up the ladder to ask if Doug could help him with his homework. He'd brought along a book that he was supposed to do a report on, and he had no idea how to go about such a thing.

Well, neither did Doug.

The two of them looked at the book for some time, holding it in their hands, turning it over and back again, studying it as a caveman might look at a cell phone if one were magically transported back in time to him.

"I got nuthin'," Doug said.

"Okay," his friend said. "I gotta go home and have dinner."

When Doug's friend got to the bottom of the ladder, Doug noticed that he had left the book behind. "Hey!" he said. "You forgot this!"

His friend glanced up and said, "Enjoy!" And then, with a devilish laugh, he knocked the ladder to the ground and ran off.

"Come back here!" Doug shouted. "Put the ladder back up!"

But his friend did not return. And before long, darkness fell.

Doug shouted and shouted for someone to come and put the ladder back up so that he could come down. But no one heard his cries for help, and this was in the days before cell phones, so Doug was on his own.

As the hours dragged on, the future premier realized he was getting a bit peckish.

Hungry, in other words.

But the tree house did not come equipped with a cupboard or fridge. There was nothing up there to eat.

Except . . . the book.

Doug waited as long as he could, but when the growling from his stomach was loud enough to drown out an overhead jet heading into Pearson, he realized he had no choice. He was *desperate*. He opened the book, tore out a couple of pages, stuffed them into his mouth, and began to chew.

"This is worse than Brussels sprouts," he said. But his hunger was so great that he kept on eating, and within a few minutes, he had eaten most of the pages, although not the cover, which was on the tough side.

It is believed to be the only book Doug Ford has ever devoured.

It was not until the following morning that a neighbour heard his cries and put the ladder back into position. The lad came down to the ground, clearly changed by what had happened to him.

He had had to resort to eating a book while trapped in a tree house.

It doesn't take Sigmund Freud to put this together. Is it any wonder that the premier, to this day, finds books "distasteful"?[43]

So, Doug has it in for libraries. He's cutting their funding. But what about trees? Why did the premier kill a plan, already in the works when he came into power, to plant fifty million trees to prevent soil erosion? That move has drawn protests from Cornwall to Sault Ste. Marie.

Well, hello? He was in a *tree house* when he had that traumatic incident.

THE GOOD NEWS

There is a silver lining to these moves.

First, libraries.

Sure, library programs are getting slashed, and laid-off librarians are being retrained as crossing guards and Walmart greeters and assassins for hire, but the good news is Ontario's libraries will not have to cut back on the number of titles that they acquire. You'll still find the same number of books on the shelves that you always did.

And you can thank Doug Ford for that.

---

43 And just what was the book the future premier had to eat? His recollection is that the book was called *The Idiocy*, and it was written by the dad character in *The Simpsons*.

He's introducing new legislation aimed at the publishing industry that will force them to only publish the first half of any work of fiction or non-fiction. Books will be half the size and therefore cost half as much.

The premier's reasoning?

"I never got to the end of a book and I don't know anyone who has," he reportedly said.

And killing the tree planting initiative?

That's actually an environmental move, believe it or not. This is all part of the Ford government's plan to reduce noise pollution.

No, it's not that trees make a lot of noise when they're growing. Don't be stupid. Think it through.

Trees get taller.

Trees have leaves.

Trees drop those leaves.

Blankets of leaves cover the province.

Leaf blowers are employed to get them to the curb.

Have you ever had to *listen* to those godawful machines? They're horrible! But as trees are culled, the need for leaf blowers will diminish, and that dreadful noise pollution will eventually be a thing of the past.

Like trees.

Says Ontario Premier Doug Ford: "You're welcome."

JUNE
21
ONTARIO PC
2019 Polls
THE LONGEST DAY

CONCLUSION

MEANWHILE, BACK IN THE THINK TANK LABORATORY . . . WHAT NEXT?

The next Ontario provincial election will be held on June 7, 2022, unless some bizarre set of circumstances drives Premier Doug Ford to call one earlier than that. This means he has the better part of two and a half years to put his stamp on Ontario and everyone who lives here.

For those Ontario voters who are not fans of this premier,[44] this is somewhat unsettling. The only thing that gets them through the day is the hope that before June 2022 rolls around, the provincial New Democrat leader, whoever that is, will soar in popularity and capture the imaginations of Ontarians. Or maybe the

---

44 Check latest census statistics for "Ontario, population."

provincial Liberals will rise from the dead, assembling someone out of spare parts gathered from previous leaders to give Doug a run for his money.

As if.

Doug is surely here to stay as long as he wants the job because Ontarians can't get enough of milquetoast MPPs, once-breathable air now laced with exhaust, larger class sizes, inadequate services for autistic children, embarrassingly tacky slogans like "buck a beer" and "open for business," fake and self-serving TV broadcasts, sex education programs from the days of *Father Knows Best*, banished overtime protections for workers, the appointment of friends to positions for which they are not qualified,[45] and pretty much daily occurrences of outright bullying.

Who wouldn't want more of that?

But what if the unthinkable were to happen? What if Doug Ford actually lost the next election? There have been some troubling signs, like when Doug was booed at the Toronto Raptors victory party, or recent polls that show the premier is slightly less popular than having a swarm of black flies in your pants.[46]

---

45 Lacrosse, anyone?

46 Doug's plummeting popularity has, however, led to one of the biggest infrastructure projects in Ontario history: rebuilding his image.

Not to worry.

Those scientists toiling away in that think tank out west? They didn't quit when they sent Doug back to seek the top job in Ontario. They are working, around the clock, to create more just like him. And not just for Ontario. They're working on "Dougs" for every province and territory in the country.

And, of course, for Ottawa.

So, rest easy. Everything's going to be fine.

And if, for some reason, these developments *do* trouble you, take heart. Just download that Tailgate Party app to your phone. It will direct you to the closest parking lot where fun-loving Ontarians are getting loaded as they rest their butts on the back bumpers of their cars.

Buck a beer never sounded better.